Alan James da Silva

EDUCATIONAL GAMES: An approach in Learning in the Teaching of Mathematics

AF209930

Alan James da Silva

EDUCATIONAL GAMES: An approach in Learning in the Teaching of Mathematics

Educational Game Applied to Mathematics

ScienciaScripts

Imprint

Any brand names and product names mentioned in this book are subject to trademark, brand or patent protection and are trademarks or registered trademarks of their respective holders. The use of brand names, product names, common names, trade names, product descriptions etc. even without a particular marking in this work is in no way to be construed to mean that such names may be regarded as unrestricted in respect of trademark and brand protection legislation and could thus be used by anyone.

Cover image: www.ingimage.com

This book is a translation from the original published under ISBN 978-620-3-46580-8.

Publisher:
Sciencia Scripts
is a trademark of
Dodo Books Indian Ocean Ltd. and OmniScriptum S.R.L publishing group

120 High Road, East Finchley, London, N2 9ED, United Kingdom
Str. Armeneasca 28/1, office 1, Chisinau MD-2012, Republic of Moldova, Europe
Managing Directors: Ieva Konstantinova, Victoria Ursu
info@omniscriptum.com

Printed at: see last page
ISBN: 978-620-3-47433-6

To God, the almighty creator of all.

DEDICATION

To my wife Leonilde Loura Albuquerque da Silva, my sons Thiago Maxsuel and Lucas Vinícius Albuquerque da Silva and my parents, José de Ribamar Pereira da Silva Sobrinho and Alzira Leódida da Silva, for the love and unrestricted support in my academic path.

2

THANKS

To my brothers Francisco das Chagas, Carlos Jorge, Gerson Laide, Carmem Célia, Alzira Filha and Márcia Carlos who were always by my side supporting me in the conclusion of one more stage.

My course group for the dedication and care needed at countless moments.

To the supervisor and esteemed professor Patrícia Alejandra Behar for all the encouragement and stimulus, providing the necessary conditions for the realization of this work.

To the masters and educators Liane Tarouco, Carlos Morais, Ana Vilma Tijiboy, Liliana M Passerino, Maira Bernardi, Rosa Maria Vicari who instructed us and transmitted their knowledge and a relationship and conviviality in all the periods of the course.

To my classmates and all of my study team, who in moments of difficulty and discouragement helped and united us in our walks that were registered in our minds.

Finally, to all those who gave me direct or indirect support for the development of this work.

"Nobody ignores everything. Nobody knows everything. We all know something. We all ignore something. So we always learn."

(Paulo Freire)

SUMMARY

The present work aims to discuss about the importance of the use of educational games in the teaching-learning process in the teaching of Mathematics in the 1st grade of High School in the Teaching Center "Aluísio Azevedo" in the city of Caxias - Maranhão, as a way of motivating the student. In addition, the technology of educational games and the use as tools of the game of mathematical reasoning in the Jungle, Tangram and TuxMath in the development of educational games will be addressed.

KEY WORDS: Educational Games; Teaching-Learning Process; Mathematics; Teaching.

SUMMARY

1 INTRODUCTION

The aim of this study is to make some reflections on the use of educational games supported by actions, to facilitate mathematical learning

The games presented in the 1st grade of High School applied in the Teaching Center "Aluísio Azevedo" in Caxias-MA using the Linux Educational operating system.

Without any pretension to exhaust the subject, it is relevant to reflect on the possibilities that arise in the classroom, exploring the resources of mathematics, as well as contextualizing with the student's everyday life.

We live in a globalised world where transformations occur at a vertiginous and uncontrollable pace. Change is something that brings innovations. However, there is a strong indication of the need for a collectivity to seek ways to improve life.

The contemporary moment has become the stage for discussions, analysis and studies on the social and educational actions of current pedagogical practices.

Consequently, the value of outlining experiences allows for the embodiment of new educational paradigms and new theories on the genesis and evolution of knowledge.

In this perspective, it is necessary the creation of didactic intervention proposals, aiming at the improvement of the teaching-learning process of the several curricular components. And in particular, the mathematics through the use of educational games, which is the object of study of the present work.

The advance of new technologies has caused a transforming impact on human life. The educational games come to revolutionize the way of teaching, its dynamics that tend to improve the teaching-learning process and provide the student a playful way of learning. This process is innovative, enabling the cognitive learning so that the education professional is prepared to master these new technologies that lead the student to think, intervene, interact, criticize and act actively in these transformations, in which "every student is always the central agent in the way he/she builds knowledge". (ANTUNES, 2003).

Educational games are means that enable an alternative technique for the evaluation of the learner. These techniques are applied to the software with obstacles where the student discovers mental calculations, the functions and the steps that will enable the dynamic process of intellectual thought of the educational game user, boosting individual or group skills depending on the degree of difficulty of the game.

In this context, playfulness, creativity, reasoning and abstraction are strengthened, which makes the learning practice a pleasurable and more significant experience in the students' education.

When studying the possibility of using a computerised game within a teaching-learning process it is necessary to consider not only its content but also the way in which the game presents itself, related to the age group of its target public.

It is also important to consider the indirect objectives that the game may provide, such as: memory (visual, auditory, kinaesthesia); temporal and spatial orientation (in two and three dimensions); psychomotor coordination (ample and fine); auditory perception; visual perception (size, colour, details, shape, position, laterality, complementation); logical-mathematical reasoning; linguistic expression (oral and written); planning and organisation, (Passerino, 1998).

For an efficient and complete use of an educational game it is necessary to previously perform a conscious evaluation of it, analysing both quality aspects of the software and pedagogical aspects, and fundamentally the pre-game and post-game situation that one wishes to achieve, (Passerino, 1998).

Aiming at a better understanding of the study, the paper is divided into four parts: the first brings the construction of the research object, in second reports a history of educational games, and then, the application of educational games in Mathematics is highlighted. Finally, a case study is presented, showing the application of game software in the Teaching Center "Aluísio Azevedo".

Within this context, the tool that enables the use of these games is the computer, which is part of the teaching-learning process that will provide the possibility of access to computers in the teacher's regency, who plans and governs the way in which he/she passes on the content to be worked on in the classroom.

> The use of the computer according to this approach makes evident each individual's learning process, which makes it possible to reflect on it in order to understand and refine it. In this way, it is possible to think of a transformation of the teaching-learning process. (ALMEIDA, 2000: p.37).

So, the computer has evidence of being a tool that facilitates the development of education in a certain process.

2 CONSTRUCTION OF THE RESEARCH OBJECT

When witnessing the scenario of education today, the pedagogical practice has undergone major changes over time time often lacking an educational plan that sees leverage a progress in education as a whole, but in the conception of the great theorists with their great theories of human development with respect to knowledge that facilitates the intellectual development of man in all phases of life. The teacher must first observe the reality of each student if the contents, methodology, and learning are adequate to the student's level of knowledge in order to achieve the desired and planned knowledge.

The teacher is responsible for directing the educational life of the student while he is in his domain and knows him very well, but looking for ways that facilitate his learning.

> One of the objectives of any good professional is to become increasingly competent in their craft. Generally, this professional improvement is achieved through knowledge and experience: knowledge of the variables involved in practice and the experience to master them. (ZABALA, 1998a)

In the teaching learning process there is a constant evaluation to measure the knowledge that is being acquired at school by the and that represents the accumulation of knowledge over time in the educational life with renewal process, currently the teacher must be able to assess the student qualitatively and quantitatively.

> [...] the qualitative assessment should   mainly take into   account the
> quality of life achieved and the involvement: In quality is not worth the
> not the extensive, but the intense; not the violent, but the involving; not pressure, but impregnation. Quality is cultural style, rather than technological; artistic, rather than productive; playful, rather than efficient; wise, rather than scientific. Therefore, it cannot be measured quantitatively, just as one cannot measure the intensity of happiness. (Pedro Demo, 1941).

10

In curricular terms the subject that will be taught together with Informatics determines the objectivity of the material to be worked is of resolutions of culture, collectivity, learning, pedagogical practice and ideology, as the education professionals are committed to education all have well defined goals, plans, attitudes and objectives so that the activities are characterised within the curricular system.

> [...] the curriculum should specify and specify the aspects of the student's personal development that should be promoted, the specific learning outcomes through which this can be achieved and the most appropriate action plan to achieve them. (SALVADOR, 1994).

The plans should be organised so as not to exhaust the content, but should be planned within the student's world, so that their learning is meaningful and they can understand what they are studying and associate it with their reality.

> [...] meaningful learning requires intense activity on the part of the student who must establish relationships between the new content
> and the elements already available in their cognitive structure". (AUSUBEL, 1968).

When it comes to educational games, it is a pedagogical material that shows the content in a more effective way for the improvement of the student reinforcing the knowledge acquired in the classroom taught by the teacher of the subject Mathematics used in connection with the computer so that it is able to contribute to student learning in a "process of rescuing the interest of the learner, in an attempt to improve their affective link with the learning situations" (Barbosa, 1998).

> [...] Educational computer games are created with the dual purpose of entertaining and enabling the acquisition of knowledge. In this context the educational computer games or simply educational games should try to explore the complete teaching-learning process. And they are great tools to support the teacher in his task, (Passerino, 1998).

The use of computational tools requires the development of specific skills of those who are directly connected to the student. Regarding pedagogical practice, it is not fundamental that the teacher only knows how to handle the resources, but it is also important that the teacher reflects on the use of these resources in education addressed in the National Curriculum Parameters - PCNs[1] and in the Law of Directives and Basis - LDB[2] (9.394/96). In this sense, the teacher can transform himself to guide his students within this new scenario.

Currently with the advent of information technology, the pedagogical practice of the teacher requires the renewal of their teaching techniques in the practical sense to be able to revolutionize the teaching-learning process "playing educates, as well as living educates: there is always something left" (LEIF 78). The use of this technology is a great challenge for the teacher and the school, because it is necessary preparation to have adequate human material for the implementation of this new way of educating and teaching, because the educational games approach a new perspective of evolution of the way of teaching.

The means to be employed in learning generate a transformation in the way of assessing. Now the assessment is made to improve the learning of students who now do not feel obliged to do it, but excited to learn something new, that is, a stage will be overcome.

This way, the results of the evaluations will be more conclusive, thus being able to direct the students to learn individually, in a way that everyone can learn. In this context, the educational games considered will be used in the Teaching Center "Aluísio Azevedo" in 1st grade.

Piaget (1966) is a great theorist who addresses a reality through research that portrays the evolutionary life in the development of the personality

---

1 National Curricular Parameters - PCNs, proposes that education is seen as a means for the development of the student allowing him/her to produce and enjoy cultural, social and economic goods and that technologies are used in education.

2 The Law of Directives and Basis - LDB (9.394/96), Article 39 brings in its caput, the importance of vocational education, integrated with the different forms of education to work and science and technology, because it will lead the learner to develop skills for productive life.

of the human being in all learning phases. In the piagetian conception, the games consist in a simple functional assimilation, in an exercise of the individual actions already learned generating, still, a feeling of pleasure for the ludic action itself and for the domain over the actions. Therefore, games have a double function: to consolidate the schemes already formed and to give pleasure or emotional balance to the child.

According to Vygotsky (VYG 89), play has an enormous influence on the development of the learner. It is through play that the student learns to act, his curiosity is stimulated, he acquires initiative and self-confidence, provides the development of language, thought and concentration.

The application of games makes it possible to create individualised teaching and learning environments (i.e. adapted to the characteristics of each student), in addition to the advantages that games bring: enthusiasm, concentration, motivation, among others. Games maintain a close relationship with knowledge construction and have influence as a motivating element in the teaching and learning process.

Basically, games are educational media that have specialised pedagogical objectives for the development of student reasoning and learning.

There are certain elements which characterise the various types of games and which can be summarised as follows: emotional involvement, spontaneity and the creativity of each player, limited time with a start, middle and end with a dynamic tone, limited space showing a fantastic world, existence of rules determining right and wrong within an imaginary world. These elements also provide the possibility of helping the student's social process by stimulating imagination, self-affirmation and autonomy.

With games it is also necessary to associate and analyse pedagogical aspects with user-machine interaction. The software developed should motivate mutual learning among the other learners who are participating in the process.

Through games, the student's memory is able to abstract what is being visualised in front of him/her on the computer, as there is a great game of concentration and memorisation.

13

This is particularly important, since for mathematics the brain can make different combinations to find the solution to the problem and difficulties posed by educational games.

3 EDUCATIONAL GAMES

An educational game is a computer program aimed at education with the purpose of assimilation of interdisciplinary contents. According to Botelho (2004), educational games are constituted by any instructional or learning format activity that involves competition and is regulated by rules and restrictions. In other words, an educational game is an application that can be used for some educational purpose and that is based on a pedagogical system.

The computer is the medium which makes the educational games viable for the appreciation of the learner who is encouraged by the teacher who becomes an instructor who mediates the teaching-learning process.

Educational games are interdisciplinary tools that transmit information and develop student learning, as they can become a motivating factor for assimilation and attention to what is presented. The observation process provided by games can make the contents clearer and more didactic, i.e. easier to assimilate.

The use of educational games together with modern forms of assessment tends to improve the teaching-learning process and provide the student with a playful way of learning. As quoted by Silveira (1998, p.02):

> games can be used for a variety of purposes within the learning context. One of the basic and very important uses is the possibility of building self-confidence. Another is to increase motivation. (...) an effective method that enables meaningful practice of what is being learned. Even the simplest of games can be used to provide factual information and practice skills, giving dexterity and competence.

In general, games have been part of our existence since the earliest ages of human history, being present not only in childhood, but also on other occasions. Games can be efficient educational tools for transmitting content, as they provide entertainment while motivating; promote learning through exercise;

15

and, improve the ability to memorise what was taught, exercising the user's mental functions and understanding.

There is a great recognition and need to have rules that identify the contextualization of how is the usability and applicability of games in everyday life of the student. This is necessary so that there is no modification of the concepts learned throughout his life, creating a new conception of the world that is in a make-believe reality.

To play using software via the computer is to be open to insecurities and to face obstacles in search of fun. Through play one discovers autonomy, creative capacity, originality and the probability of simulating and getting to know threatening and forbidden circumstances in everyday reality.

It is essential to emphasize the usability of technological resources, where educational games must be previously analyzed and studied, so that there is knowledge of the operation by the teacher to use as a pedagogical means in the classroom to his pupils. It is important that the game is linked to objective and well-founded theoretical and methodological principles. For this, the teacher must know a lot about the handling of new technologies and should make a careful and judicious analysis of the material aiming at the objective to be achieved before using them.

The ultimate issue is to transform users of educational games into thinkers capable of abstracting concepts and situations. Currently there is a great exponent of dissemination of educational games: the Internet. In this context, the school should be responsible for making this kind of knowledge available in a creative way to the school community, that is, to divulge the educational games as ludic stimulators of the development of the teaching-learning process.

According to Vygotsky (VYG 89), play has an enormous influence on child development. It is through play that the student learns to act, his curiosity is stimulated, he acquires initiative and self-confidence, and provides for the development of language, thought and concentration.

Also according to Vygotsky (VYG 89), educational games help to pass on to the learner the learning that will be useful for school education. In Piaget's conception (FAR 95), games consist in a simple functional assimilation, in an exercise of the individual actions already learned, generating, still, a feeling of pleasure for the ludic action itself and for the domain over the actions. Therefore, games have a double function: to consolidate the schemes already formed and to give pleasure or emotional balance to the learner.

Educational games are classified according to their objectives in: action, adventure, casino, logical, strategic, sports, among others according to (Tarouco, 2004). Their educational application may vary according to their classification. For example, action games can be used in the motor development of younger students who are developing concentration, eye-hand organization and help in the process of quick thinking in sudden situations.

From a pedagogical point of view, the ideal is that the game should alternate between occasions of cognitive activities and motor agility practice.

Adventure games are responsible for the user's mastery of the atmosphere to be discovered. When well modelled pedagogically, it can help in the simulation of activities with a more complex degree of difficulty to be experienced in the classroom, such as an ecological accident or a chemical experiment, (Tarouco, 2004).

Logic games create challenges, demanding more from the intellect than from the reflexes. This type of game is usually timed, that is, there is a time limit that must be obeyed by the user in the execution of his task. For example, classic games such as drama, chess, or a simple word search may require reasoning that can be timed, (Tarouco, 2004).

Educational games are gaining more and more space in the ludic dimensions, bringing to the user sensations of pleasantness and comfort, given that the student assumes an active position interacting with what the game presents.

Although educational games are an important playful tool, their application is by no means random. When analysing the probability of using a game within a teaching methodology, other aspects, besides its content, should be taken into consideration. For example, one should consider whether the game presents information in a clear way, and if it is appropriate to the age of the target audience to which you want to apply the educational game.

At the same time it is important to analyse the indirect objectives that the game can develop in the pupil, such as: stimulating the visual, auditory and kinaesthetic memory; the brain; the required motor coordination; adequate logical-mathematical intelligence; and, if oral and written linguistic expression is well planned and organised.

For a competent and complete use of an educational game it is necessary to make a conscious assessment of it beforehand, analysing both the software's characteristics and the pedagogical aspects involved. Essentially it is necessary to evaluate the pre-game and post-game situation that one aims to achieve, according to Passerino (1998).

In other words, one should avoid anything that might change the student's focus. In fact, the application of games is directly related to the age of the students who will use them. Learning through gestures and repetition of movements can be done from kindergarten to adulthood. At ages between 7 and 12, the computer becomes an important tool for working on reasoning. When the game has rules, it also begins to have an eminent social character, and can be applied from childhood to adulthood. The latter include games such as football (sensory-motor) [3]and chess (intellectual).

The activities performed during the execution of a game can mobilise brain schemes that stimulate thought, order time and space interacting in various dimensions of the affective, social, motor and cognitive personality, favouring the acquisition of cognitive conducts and the performance of agilities such as organisation, speed, exercise, strength, concentration, among others.

The advantages of using games in education is the possibility of forming virtues such as mutual respect, participation, obedience to rules, prudence, responsibility, justice, individual and collective initiative. The educational game

---

3 (Piaget, 1966).

is the connection that unites aspiration and pleasure during the performance of an activity. Teaching using playful means creates a rewarding and fascinating atmosphere that serves as a stimulus for the integral development of the student.

Currently, computer games for education should present virtual representations with styles consistent with the reality of the student, providing large amounts of information presented in different ways, such as images, text, sounds, movies, and the information should be shown clearly and following a logic.

In the realization of the game activities, the user is allowed to check the effect of their performance immediately, promoting a self-correction founding the individual esteem of the same, creating a spatial alignment of data expressed when manipulating the educational game. In the usability of the game, the student must have patience in repeating the activities proposed by the game to stimulate cognitive, sensory and motor skills. The repetition may allow the stimulation of the learner's inventive capacity, encouraging the intellectual growth, since the student will not worry about the possible mistakes that may arise during the teaching-learning process.

In summary, the advantages that make the use of educational games facilitating learning feasible are:

a) Clarity

b) Concentration

c) Motivation

d) Measuring intelligence

e) Stimulates learning development

f) Awakens playfulness (activity: playing and learning)

g) Attention-grabbing

h) Develops cognitive reasoning, etc.

Despite all the playful possibilities, there are still obstacles in the use of educational games, because games that work with more complex concepts such as trigonometry and probability are still scarce, if not non-existent. Moreover, the big problem is still that competition can distract the student's attention from the concept involved in the game.

With the popularity of the World Wide Web, it has become possible to create new forms that support education through play, such as Internet games. This allows the computer to be used for online interaction in different regions of the world. The school should be equipped with computers and connected to the world wide web for the use of interactive games. Currently, the use of games on the Web is increasing. Teachers can now use these games in their lessons to simulate, educate and advise. However, care should be taken with motivation, especially if the learner is not interested in solving the game, making it boring. The connection speed should also be a factor to be considered, since a low *download* speed can make the process tedious and demotivating.

The usability of these new learning media changes the teaching dynamics, the strategies and the obligations of the learner and the teachers regarding the responsibility of each one in the teacher-student interaction process. With this, the new media and tools that serve as support for education can grow significantly, generating a dynamic and motivating learning.

The interactive game, as a rule, follows a pattern according to the age group of the learner. In this context, difficulty levels develop and knowledge about what is being discussed is fixed more easily. The game in general creates a very high expectation in the user, who sees it holds your attention to what is new, ie, stimulates what is in the following phases, for this reason the game becomes interesting, motivating and enlightening.

4 EDUCATIONAL GAMES APPLIED TO MATHEMATICS

Educational games can considerably modify the way of learning and teaching in the classroom. In the context of this work, educational games are used to work mathematical concepts. These concepts are worked through logical and deductive reasoning operations, being applied in the 1st series of High School of Basic Education.

> ...] in our daily lives we use various forms of play: that of the senses, in which curiosity leads us to knowledge; the body games expressed in dance in the ceremonies and rituals of certain peoples; the game of colours, form and sounds, present in the art of the immortals; the game of looking. In short, it is there, making art of our lives. The intensity of the power of play is so great that no science has been able to explain the fascination it exerts over people, Martins (2002, p.1).

The games are in various sectors of human life as corporal and ritual expression from collective games to individual games using various forms of tools from the various types of balls to computer games expressed in all its utilities that fascinates man with affirms Martins.

The games in a general way follow the evolution of the knowledge of the humanity until being used in a classroom as a teaching-learning process in a subject that has the numbers and geometric figures as its main functionality which is Mathematics working in connection with Informatics.

The games discussed work on the interdisciplinarity between Mathematics and Computer Science using an Educational Linux operating system.

The Educational Linux system is a compilation of Linux based on the Unix system that was developed by a Finnish student called Linux Torvalds on October 5, 1991 and that through the original Linux the technicians of the

Ministry of Education - MEC developed a Brazilian system with a graphical interface with applications with games, graphics and other programs that make up the Educational Linux Operating System to meet the Federal, State and Municipal public schools.

For the application of these games in the grades, mathematical formulas used depart from the everyday life of each student. For the case studies three educational games are used, whose objectives are, especially, to help concentration, attention and increase the student's interest in learning mathematics. The games considered are: Math in the Jungle, Tangram and TuxMath. Each one has peculiarities that make them attractive to the students.

The attractiveness of the games awakens emotional sensations, which can lead the user to an experience of appreciation, creating motivation to face circumstances provided by the mentioned games. It is valuable to use the games as pedagogical didactic means in the teaching-learning process, not just approaching the game for the game's sake but considering it as a powerful working tool. As already mentioned, the computerized educational games have as purpose the entertainment and the availability of new knowledge, reinforcing the desire to discover what in its next levels.

For Passerino (1998) highlights some elements that qualify educational games cites below:

The ability to absorb the user intensely and totally, to maintain a mood, feeling of exaltation and tension and at the same time with joy and distraction will develop:

a) Emotional involvement;

b) Spontaneity and creativity;

c) The time limitation. In the game there is a beginning, middle and end, with a dynamic character.

d) The space limitation is temporary and fantastic;

e) Existence of rules;

With the existence of rules, these elements must be worked out in the execution of the game so that there is a balance and coherence in the use of computer resources. Moreover, these elements must be adjusted so as to benefit the learner, facilitating the understanding of the content that will be worked on in the educational game.

In this context, there are many other educational games aimed at teaching Mathematics that have advantages for the cultural, social, intellectual and cognitive development of the student. Among the main ones we can mention Math Memory, Tabuada *Tetris,* Math Track, GL Market, *PacMan*, Math GP and SuperMemory. On the other hand, there are games that involve action and violence, like *Quake, Doom, Carmagedon, as* well as strategy or speed games like *Age of Empires*, *Rise of Nations*, *Age of Mithology* and *Need for Speed*. Other titles are also popular with teenagers and adults, such as *Tetris* and *FreeCell*. These are games that can assist the teacher and are specific to education that should be used in the teaching-learning process with educational gaming.

In other words, when using the game is necessary a pre-assessment of its operation to avoid possible failures, as already discussed in Chapter 3. In this evaluation, it is essential to observe from the user interaction interface, analyzing pedagogical aspects and the quality of the program, to the situation before the game (pre-game) and after the game (post-game) to achieve what you want.

Learning through games brings motivation, and this learning is practiced both individually and cooperatively (in group). "The educational games can awaken in the student: motivation, stimulus, curiosity, interest in learning (...) the student builds his knowledge in a playful and pleasurable way" Silveira (1998).

Taking this statement into consideration, evidence of these elements will be sought in the games Math in the Jungle, Tangram and TuxMath. The choice of these educational games was due to the fact that they are focused on the learning of mathematics, through concentration and logical reasoning, which are appropriate for the aforementioned grades.

23

4.1 The Maths in the Jungle Educational Game

The Jungle Math Game aims to develop concentration and memorization. The player must work with various mathematical operations, such as: addition, subtraction, multiplication, division, potentiation, radication and numerical expressions, and these operations form the challenges and obstacles that must be overcome.

Several players, previously registered, can participate in the game, and the players will become small frogs that must go through the path provided by the board. If necessary, the game provides guidance on how to play, as well as offering the possibility of an interdisciplinary process, because besides motivating the learning of the four fundamental operations, it works a healthy competition in the classroom, through values such as partnership and quick thinking to interpret the situations suggested in the game.

In addition, it is important to note that two players is the minimum number of participants, while the maximum number is six. To walk around the board, the player must roll a die, and a question is asked according to the position reached.

The board and an example expression can be seen in Figure 1. The expression must be solved within forty seconds, otherwise the player returns to the previous position.

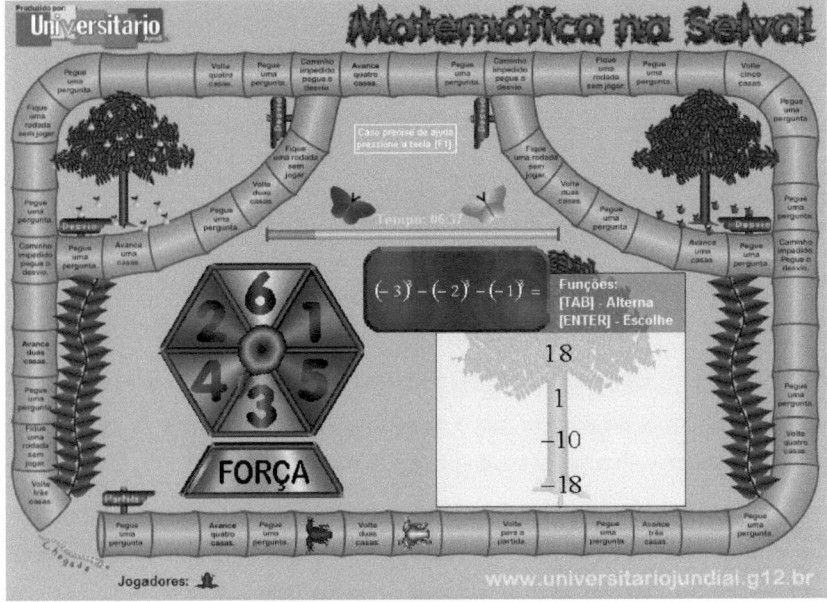

Figure 1: Mathematics in the Jungle

As can be seen the Math in the Jungle game can be considered as collective learning. As it limits the time to solve the problem it also contributes to increase the speed of arithmetic reasoning.

4.2 Tangram educational game

The Tangram game is a game invented by the Chinese that works logical reasoning, perception, motivation, spatial memory, playfulness, stimulating interest and attention. The game features four levels with various levels as can be seen in Figure 2.

25

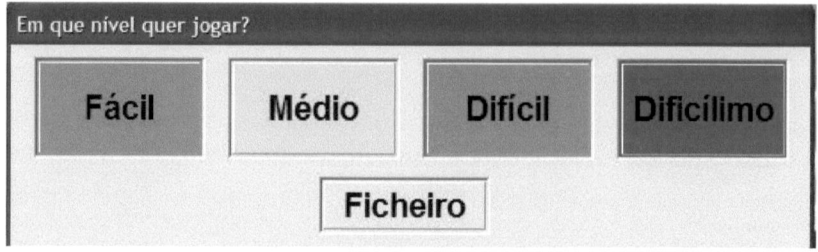

Figure 2: The Tangram game

Tangram is an ancient game of shapes, whose objective is to create a particular shape with a set of seven pieces, forming a puzzle.

In each puzzle the goal is to place the pieces that are on the right side of the screen, and the pieces cannot overlap. If the problem is not solved the user can ask for help for this task. Each level presents different types of figures, an example of the easiest level is shown in Figure 3 and an example of a difficult and complex figure is shown in Figure 4.

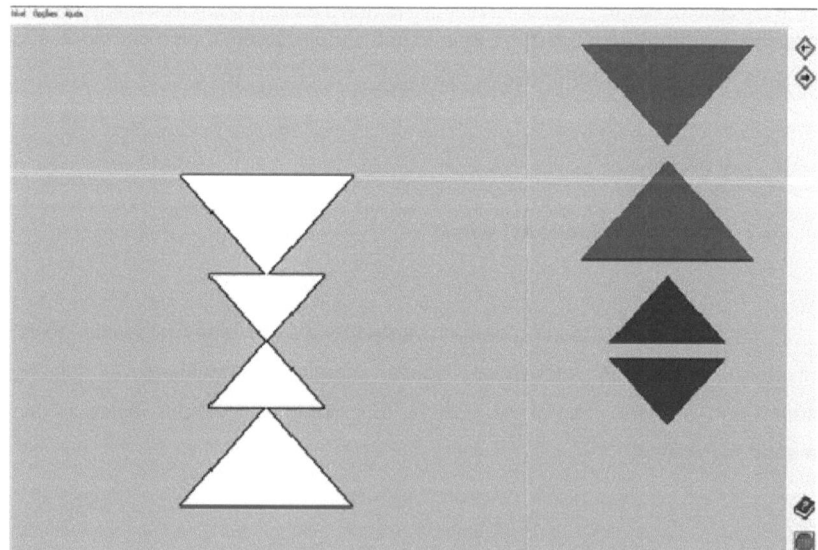

Figure 3: 1st level 1st phase - Tangram

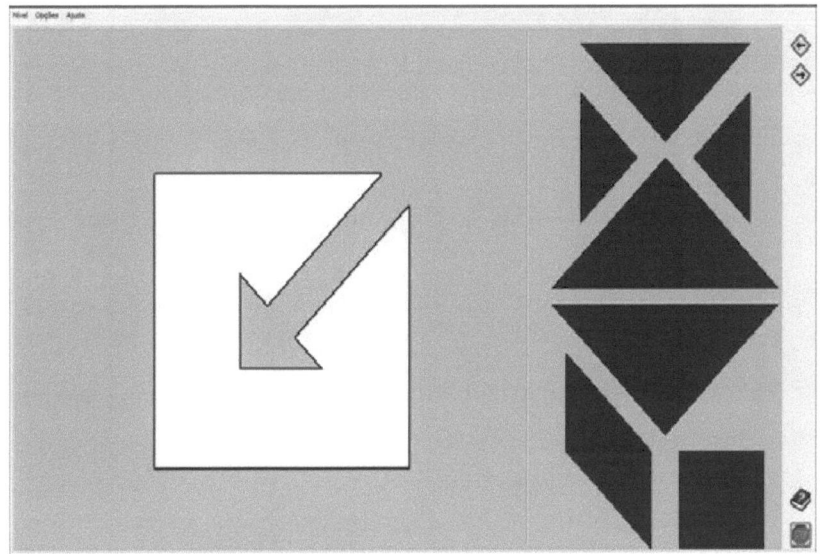

Figure 4: 1st stage of the very difficult level

As can be observed Tangram is a game that demands a lot from the geometric ability (2D) of the students. In this context, the game provides a gradual training in the geometric field in two dimensions.

4.3 The TuxMath game

This type of game explores the student's attention, perception, concentration and agility, and works with several phases that determine the complexity of each operation presented. The operations available in the game are arithmetic operations, that is, the user will have to perform addition, subtraction, multiplication and division of natural numbers. Through this game the student will be able to acquire quick reasoning by being presented with calculations continuously. Figure 5 illustrates some operations that must be calculated;

27

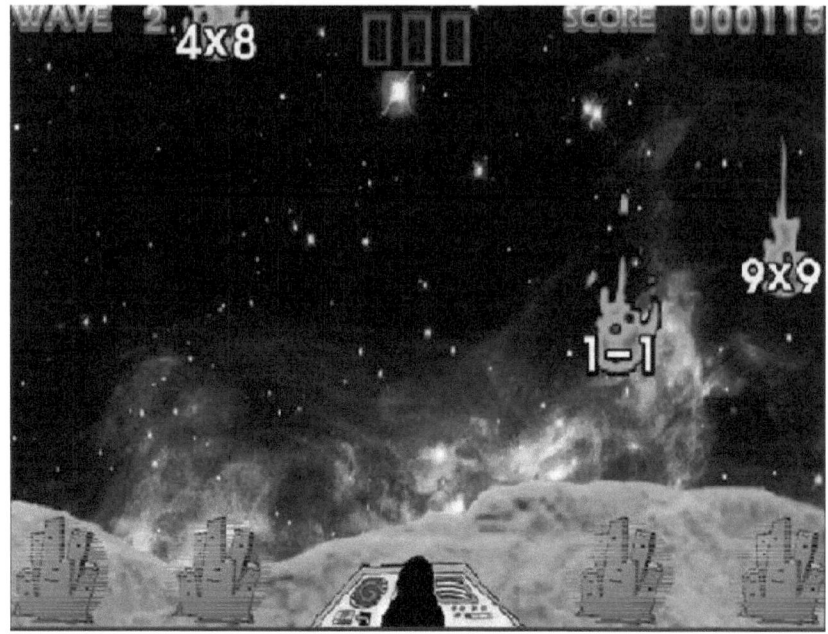

Figure 5: TuxMath game phase

In the first and second stage of the game operations appear in a slow manner. The goal is to destroy the accompanying asteroids and save the buildings on the ground. As the student moves through the stages the asteroids fall at a higher speed, which forces the student to process the required operations faster. When an operation is done correctly the asteroid is destroyed. This type of educational game can be considered as memorization, because the learner is learning by repetition.

With the presentation of the games considered, Chapter 4 deals with the case study where the games are applied.

5 METHODOLOGY

What was presented in the previous chapters, the teaching-learning process is to work the student in a satisfactory way in discovering his abilities and aptitudes, with curricular contents, with a learning that adapts him to the reality experienced in the daily life, so that he has a quality and equal educational environment. The teacher must have lived experiences of teaching as an example that can be followed as resources for improving the teaching that leads the learner to learn in a meaningful way.

In this context, the chapter presents a methodology in which we work with the objectives that were applied in the 1st year of High School in the Teaching Centre Aluisio Azevedo - Caxias - MA, making an interdisciplinary between Computer Science with Mathematics, whose methodology can be adapted and applied in other subjects used the areas of computer science.

The steps will be followed according to the proposed methodology as they will be detailed in the following steps.

5.1 Idealisation and lesson planning

In this stage, the plan is to define the pedagogical activities that will be worked by the pupils, as a priority the subjects taught in the classroom or in a previous classroom to the pupils of the 1st grade classes, in view of a survey on a pre-requisite already observed, whose contents have already been approached, in which they will take part as hypothesis and reference point for learning.

In this process, the teacher must be able to identify his or her intentions towards the students, or that he or she wants the students to achieve good learning and which objective should be reached by the student he or she proposes to develop.

Learn to analyze the educational game (software), after some explanations, definitions starting from some knowledge about computer games aimed at Mathematics, exemplifying the geometric figures, the fundamental operations, numerical expressions, potentiation, radications, number sets, etc. The teacher recommends that students view the activities revealed in each game established in the five grades of the 1st grade previously defined for use of the operating system Educational Linux that during the year was worked educational computing to then apply activity in a defined time for the development of the execution of the game.

The teacher will know what he or she has developed and planned during the lessons in each grade and what objective has been achieved because the students are able to manipulate the educational game that will help them develop the activities of the subject in the classroom using a computer program facilitating the teaching-learning process both in the classroom and in the laboratory using computers as well as books.

5.2 Gathering information and materials required

With the help of the regular teacher, the students acquire information that will clarify the content to be worked on in the lab as a review to reinforce the deeper subjects that will be covered in the joint classroom, such as 1st and 2nd crane functions, modular and exponential functions. This data is collected directly under the guidance of the educator who will help the student with the new content presented in the annual plan.

For better understanding, we use an example from a Maths lesson, the teacher may require students to know geometric figures, some types, whether it is a regular or irregular polygon to be identified and drawn in the notebook.

To begin with, it can be presented to the students subjects that must be studied in the 5th to 8th grade primary schools books as a notion and review of the subject that will be studied in the classroom for that is used a software of an educational game related to mathematics, then make an investigation of the content if it is appropriate to then apply to the students about flat figures. After all, the educator will guide the development of a review activity for a diagnosis of the knowledge acquired over the years as a student in previous classes that helped develop a learning that supports the teaching of mathematics for students can associate the content covered in class. This form of learning brings skill in the knowledge of numbers.

5.3   Carrying out the activities

This is followed by an organisation or timetable of activities to be developed and carried out by the student. It is the stage in which the student shows his abilities of what he has learned by expressing his knowledge, identifying what he has learned and what is necessary to deepen the knowledge. The educator must analyze the student's development if they are learning, with respect to classes if they are stimulating them intellectually so they can functionalize their skills and competencies, given that the error, the analysis is a starting point for a new beginning to can solve problems that always arise in the teaching learning process, for this it is essential to solve the errors and find concrete answers "learn to err, to analyze the error and make it a valid hypothesis for the search for new hypotheses. (BUSTAMANTE 1987 apud OLIVEIRA, 2002).

5.4 Verification of learning

How true is the depth of what has been learned? To reach the target of a real and meaningful learning, it is necessary the maturity of the intellectual growth. In order for this not to happen it is necessary to have elements and resources which develop significantly the teaching-learning process in the student's life.

It is observed that this methodological step is carried out step by step during the process of exercising the lessons, in the course of activities the master evaluates student performance in valuing learning as the initial goal, this happens to discover students who are having difficulty assimilating the content. In the face of this process, if the teacher has not achieved its objective, it should make a retrospective of goals and attitudes and study and develop means that can be applied to improve student learning "Piaget's work leads to the conclusion that the work of educating does not refer to the transmission of content as much as to promote the student's mental activity. (PIAGET, p. 55-57 apud REVISTA NOVA ESCOLA, 2003).

The methodology is divided as follows firstly it presents the understanding and execution of the educational games (software) Mathematics in the Jungle, Tangram and Tuxmath with configuration of the transformation of the repository of adaptations for Educational Linux and secondly the educational games listed the operations of addition, subtraction, multiplication, division, potentiation, radiciation, rationalization, study of radicals, numerical expressions, plane and geometric figures, numerical sets with basis for the study of sets, intervals, relations, functions of 1st and 2nd degree, modular and exponential function, in order to build a motivating and pleasurable scenario seeking to streamline the teaching of mathematics.

6 CASE STUDY: APPLICATION OF THE GAMES

6.1 Introduction

The research project is considered interdisciplinary and involves the disciplines of Mathematics and Computer Science. The computer programmes used are educational games (Mathematics in the Jungle, Tangram and TuxMath).

The subject was taught at the "Aluísio Azevedo" Teaching Centre in the computer lab with the five first year high school classes in the morning shift at their respective times.

6.2 Instrument and Methodology

6.2.1 Activity planning

The research project had great pedagogical importance for the development of the school considered as a whole, especially in the Mathematics subject, since a significant change in student learning was perceived.

The activities developed in the investigative process with the target audience: teachers and students began in December 2008.

The planning occurred as would be developed the classes followed starting from the content of revisional character on basic issues to the program of the first series, whose content already mentioned in the previous chapter. Considering that the classes were expository, dialogued and interactive directly using computer.

6.2.2 School data collection

In the school field it was found that there is a large contingent of teachers of an excellent intellectual level who work for the improvement of education as a whole, which perform work that enable the emergence of new pedagogical form of renewal that takes knowledge to the student always, in a motivating and egalitarian process. In this approach, it is emphasized the option to make this research project in the perspective of streamlining the study of mathematics, looking for mechanism that helps to further improve education in this educational establishment, having a sample picture of a reality currently to be innovative example in the relentless pursuit in the development of knowledge that serves as a model for other schools in the state network.

The case study aims to accompany the development of Mathematics Teaching, helping the student's cognitive, psychological and intellectual growth as a mediation of the pedagogical actions taken by the regular teacher who knows the student's reality and who has a work focused on teaching-learning with the application of educational games

Another focus of the research was to detect possible deficiencies of memorization or fiction on the part of the student in learning mathematics, thus allowing to know the development of students facing the challenges of the discipline in practice using the computer as an educational tool that allows the display of knowledge through information of the content covered in the classroom by the teacher.

The investigative work also includes a survey on the pedagogical practice of the teacher and the student with respect to the usability of computers and computer games.

We also investigated the school's staff, which consists of more than one hundred (100) teachers, most of whom have higher education qualifications and work 20 to 40 hours a week. Currently the school has approximately 1075 students.

6.2.3 Gathering information and materials required

At this stage the students could observe, analyse and research the information passed on about the content seen in the classroom and then relate what the educational games were presenting to the educational reality of each student, with guidance from the teacher.

Then, the students developed the activities used the games that approached the operations of addition, subtraction, multiplication, division, potentiation, radiciation, rationalization, plane and geometric figure, numerical sets until finding the solution of each game. The students are free to play manipulating the computer program, to understand how the system behaves, adapting the reality of each student with the conditions of the game that were presented in the execution of the same associated to several circumstances found in practice.

6.2.4 Pedagogical aspects

It was observed that the computer lab has 10 computers with the operating system Educational Linux, two air conditioners, a central table, four benches. The laboratory also has a printer, an acrylic board, a 29" television and three teachers distributed in the morning, afternoon and evening shifts.

Regarding the pedagogical and curricular aspects, the school has a Political Pedagogical Project (PPP) [4]whose objective is to improve the quality of education based on the Law of Directives and Bases of Education (LDB) and National Curriculum Parameters (PCN) preparing students for citizenship, being critical and responsible to perform their education outside school with quality.

---

4 The Political Pedagogical Project (PPP) are educational guidelines that are committed to the formation of critical, participative, responsible, committed and creative citizens.

6.3 Teachers

The sample is represented below by the graphs that portray the reality of a contingent of approximately 100 teachers. The following presentation will be addressed first to the reality of the teachers of the Teaching Center "Aluísio Azevedo" in order to know the degree of credibility of educational games before the educators of the initial classes of high school in the morning shift.

The research conducted with teachers aimed to perform a diagnosis of the framework on the level of acceptance of educational games itself. In this approach, its usability, interaction and interactivity at school is fundamental as a motivating process, assimilating with a renovating methodological procedure, which better visualises the understanding of the contents of a certain discipline.

The charts will reveal the situation of teachers and students of the Teaching Center "Aluísio Azevedo" in the city of Caxias - MA. The questionnaire used regarding the teachers can be seen in Appendix 1.

The research shows that the teaching staff is well qualified in terms of the courses from which they are graduated, however, there is no undergraduate teacher who is teaching, but most of them are in a process of continuous training,

Reality shows that education needs more qualified professionals so that they can be up to date to face the transformations and trends as shown in Figure 6, which depicts the professional training of teachers in percentage terms according to the data provided during the survey. The teachers' level of knowledge is of great value in terms of content and didactics in the pedagogical process.

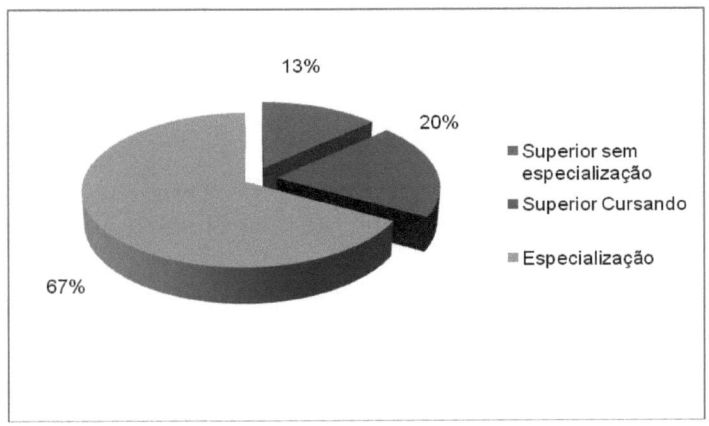

13%

20%

67%

- Superior sem especialização
- Superior Cursando
- Especialização

Figure 6: Vocational training

In Figure 6 it can be seen that all teachers have at least completed higher education 13% (thirteen percent) have no specialisation, 67% (sixty seven percent) have specialisation and a percentage of 20% (twenty percent) are in the process of completing a postgraduate course. This can evidenced that there is a certain concern with teaching since the sum total of the diagnosis 87% (eighty-seven percent) are seeking knowledge beyond graduation.

It is interesting to note that 60% (sixty percent) have more than ten years dedicated to teaching, while 33% (thirty-three percent) responded that they work in the period of six to nine years and 7% (seven percent) between one and five years. It is clearly observed from the data that no teacher has less than one year teaching experience as revealed in the graph in Figure 7.

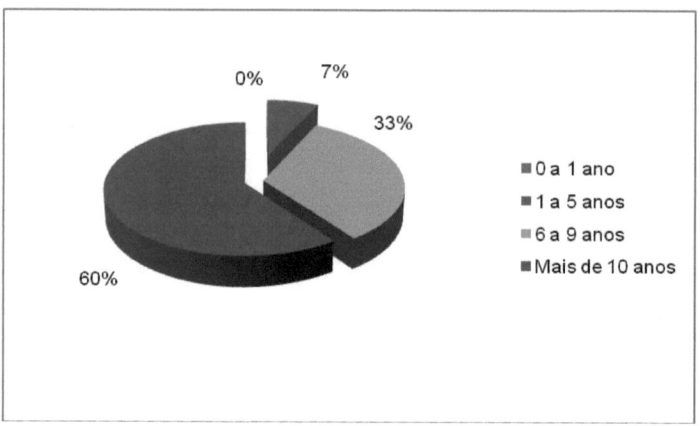

Figure 7: Length of Service

In fact, getting students' attention and making them learn faster is one of the challenges of the educational process. In this context, games appear as a tool to achieve these objectives, and although this is true, none of the teachers who participated in the research have ever applied games in their classes. The games, in fact, should be used to enrich the classes, not to replace the teacher, that is, the student should use the computer as a learning tool, but through the awareness of the masters of all for use significantly improve the in the formation of the student as a whole.

Of all the teachers interviewed, they consider the application of educational games in the teaching-learning process important, given that games can be used as a facilitating element in this process. According to the teachers, the games develop logical reasoning skills and stimulate curiosity.

Although games were considered important, the teachers who took part in the survey found that many education professionals have knowledge about computers, as shown in Figure 8. Of the participants, only 20% (twenty per cent) claimed to have a knowledge of computing. Sixty percent (60%) said they have regular knowledge about the use of computing. The remaining 13% (thirteen percent) have only basic knowledge about computer. Another point is 7% (seven percent) have no knowledge about computer only notions.

38

The graph shows that teacher qualification in relation to computing should be constant. On the other hand, it can also be observed that all teachers believe it is necessary to have computer knowledge in order to use educational games.

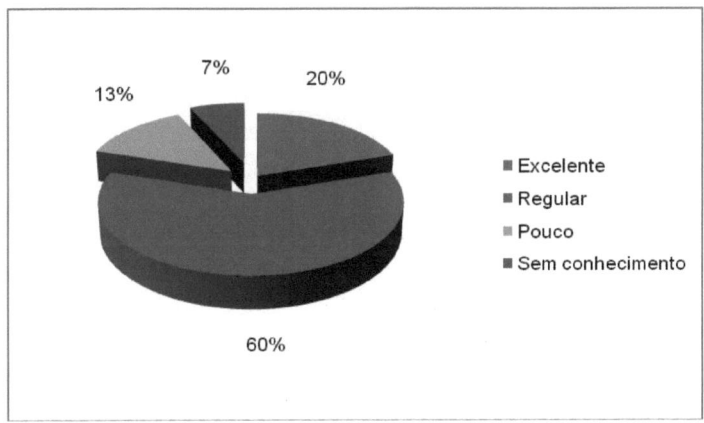

Figure 8: Computer literacy

Figure 9 shows a picture of teachers' knowledge about computer games. In the graph shown, 67% (sixty-seven percent) stated that they already have knowledge about computer games aimed not at education with the purpose of entertainment, and the remaining 33% (thirty-three percent) i.e. a good part have no knowledge about digital games, revealing the need for further dissemination of the playful use of games.

The computer is the tool that assists the teacher in passing on content in the teaching-learning process for all stages of education in the life of the student who becomes the main transforming agent in this educational process that is responsible for transmitting knowledge.

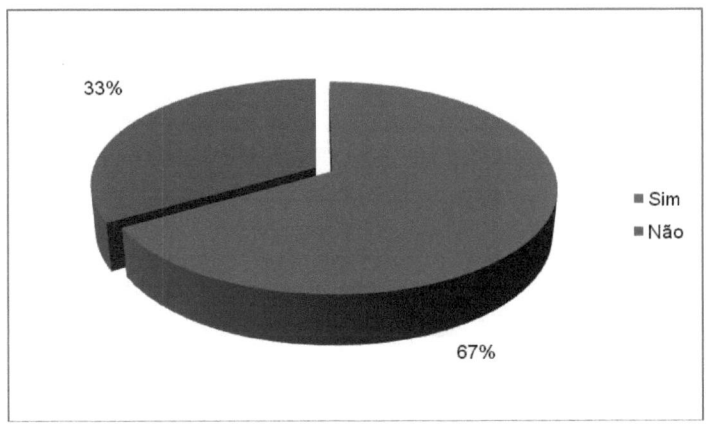

Figure 9: Knowledge about computer games.

With regard to knowledge of games focused on education, Figure 10 of the survey showed that teachers are aware that it is feasible to use software that links the subject taught in the classroom with computers to improve teaching. The graph in the figure shows a percentage of 57% (fifty-seven percent) that education professionals are aware of educational games, while 43% (forty-three percent) do not know about this type of game.

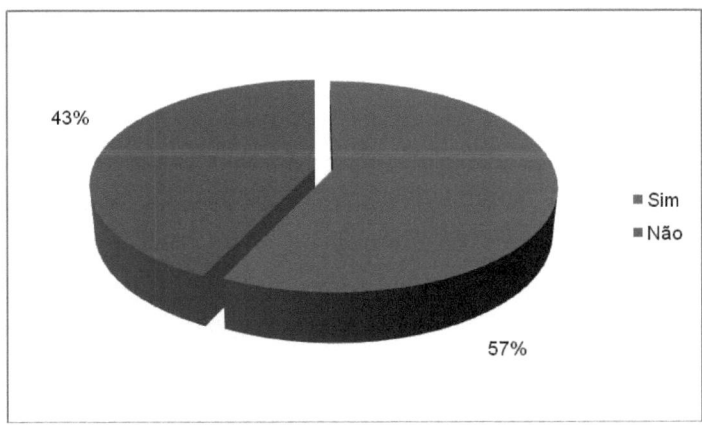

Figure 10: Some knowledge about educational gaming.

Teachers were asked what knowledge they felt was necessary for students to be able to use games. In this questioning, 33% (thirty-three percent) agreed that for proper use of educational games in the computer lab, it is necessary for students to have basic notions of computing. It was also noted that 47% (forty-seven percent) of teachers believe that knowledge about the educational game software presented in the Educational Linux operating system, to be applied should be seen in the school itself, in other words, that this knowledge should be acquired through learning projects. Given that the use of the internet is required, 20% (twenty percent) agreed that knowledge of the internet and the software are required to use the software.

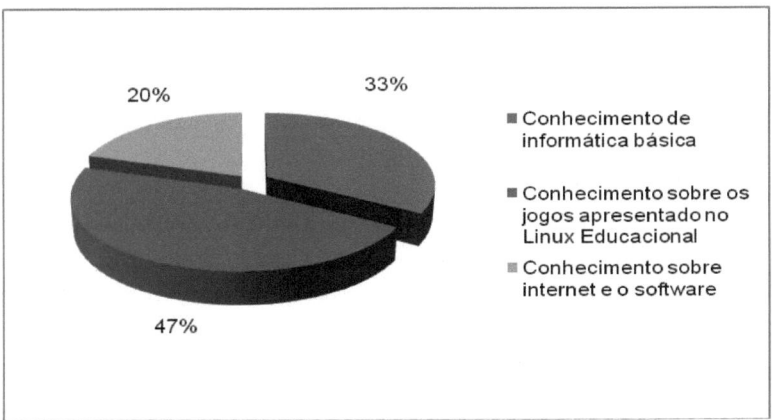

Figure 11: What do you consider important for the appropriate use of educational games in
computer lab with high school students.

The research revealed the qualification of the work developed by the teacher of Computer Science with the use of educational games interdisciplinary with Mathematics before the students and other teachers of the school that was a percentage shown in figure 12, the result of 61% (sixty-one percent) agreed that the teaching practice of the teacher of Computer Science good, 23% (twenty-three percent) found it very good, 8% (eight percent) recognized that the work developed is excellent and important for the improvement of the teaching of Mathematics and 8% (eight percent) did not know what is being developed at school.

41

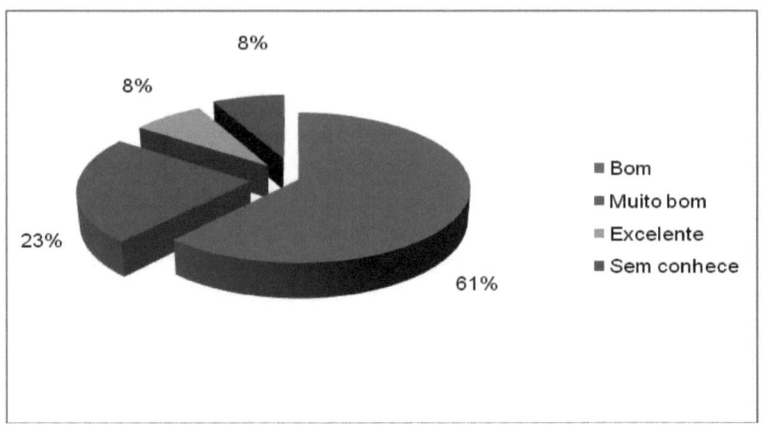

Figure 12: Quality of the work developed at school with the use of games

As already mentioned, the computer today (using digital games) is fundamental for learning, especially considering it as a factor generating interactivity and affectivity, favouring the resolution of activities linked to Mathematics or any other subject. In this context, teachers were questioned regarding the use of games as a motivating factor; the results (Figure 13) showed that 23% (twenty-three percent) found games to be a good motivation for students, they increase their power of concentration. Thirty-one percent (31%) rated this process as very good for the development of education at school. Forty-six percent (46%) of respondents saw games as excellent for use in the classroom. No interviewee considered the application of games as bad.

The principle of motivation was presented by Piaget improves student learning in the face of obstacles by making the same solve the problem, thus the master will have success in its proposed objectives in the constant search for knowledge in the teaching process.

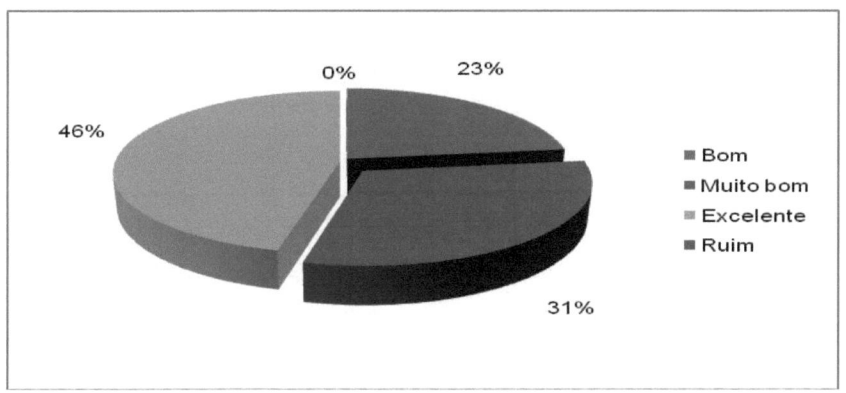

Figure 13: The use of the computer in learning with educational games that aim to motivate, increase the power of concentration, favouring the resolution of activities.

After the application of the games it was verified how the teachers self-assessed themselves regarding their knowledge about games. Figure 13 presents the new results.

Although some teachers knew something about educational games, only 31% (thirty-one percent) had ever applied some kind of game (computer game or not) to motivate the student, as can be seen in Figure 14. A significant percentage of 69% (sixty-nine percent) had no knowledge of educational games, although many answered that they knew many of these games.

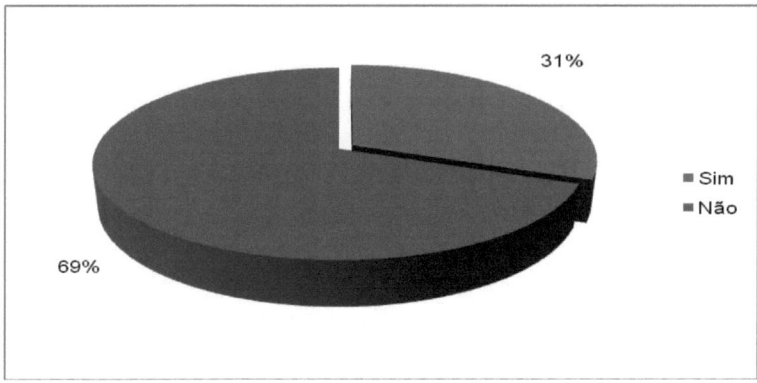

Figure 14: Application of some game in the classroom by the teacher.

As seen in Figure 14, the results are extremely relevant when teachers were asked about the applicability of a game in the classroom. This diagnosis justifies the need to work with games in the classroom.

Figure 15 shows that 23% (twenty-three percent) of the teachers interviewed are concerned that the student needs to go beyond books and notebooks, i.e., that educational games are a possibility to assist student learning, but have used some game outside the classroom as a form of distraction. On the other hand, 77% (seventy-seven percent) never used a game outside the classroom and replied that this procedure is regular, since they had already heard of the existence of this new way of socializing knowledge in the teaching-learning process.

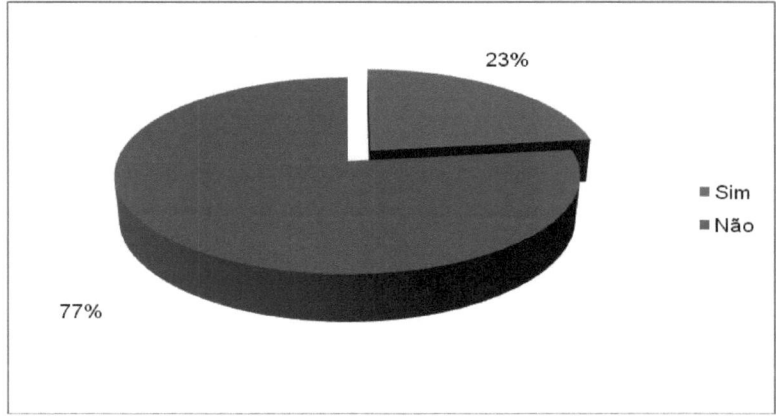

Figure 15: The student needs activities other than those provided in books and notebooks.

6.4 Pupils

For the analysis and interpretation of the collected data, research methods and instruments were used, such as: a questionnaire addressed to the students asking about the use of educational games, aiming to assess the usability of the games considered in this work.

The questioning involved aspects related to the students, such as gender, date of birth and the grade they study. Other questions were prepared with the aim of identifying the satisfaction of the student with the game used. The survey also had the participation of teachers who collaborated with the research.

The data collection considered aspects present in the games such as colours, scenarios, tips and opinions of changes suggested by the students involved in the process. Also in the research were worked the aspects that highlighted the attraction in each student in the games used.

Regarding the situation of difficulties found in the execution of the games, the graphics highlight that approximately 65 students of approximately 190 of all the series in question cited in the project, have understood the control alternatives provided by the tool regarding the execution of a new game with new operations created with greater obstacles, besides the time given for the manipulation of the games and the penalties caused by the actions required in the operations provided.

In the game Math in the Jungle, the participants had difficulties in answering the questions due to the operations made to think. These difficulties are reported to be due to several factors such as: lack of practice due to mastering the handling of the computer, understanding the language intended for a target audience within their ages.

Regarding, the analysis to the games scenario and the components, many students reported that they liked the colours, sounds and the questions, being this one of the main points of attraction, because the games present customization of colours in the environment that is satisfactory to all.

This section presents the results related to the students when they used the educational games. As described in Chapter 4, the games considered were: Tangram, TuxMath and Math in the Jungle. The questionnaire regarding the students of the five morning shift classes is presented in Appendix 2.

The students in these classes are adolescents who already have a level of knowledge formed in class about mathematics. These subjects include

45

fractions, addition, subtraction, multiplication, division, potentiation, radiation, radicals, numerical expressions and notions about number sets.

Regarding the age of the participants, they are in the age range between 15 and 21 years and above. Students between 15 and 16 are 48% (forty eight percent), between 17 and 18 are 41% (forty one percent) of students. Between 19 and 20 the percentage is 8%, (eight percent) being that of 21 years above constitutes only 3% (three percent), with reference to the participants 46% (forty six percent) were male and 54% (fifty four percent). Through these results it can be observed that students already possess a certain maturity[5] which is important for the development of learning (Piaget, apud [FAR 95]).

Intelligence[6] is worked in any age group, in the formation of personality and development of learning in any Discipline (Vygotsky, apud [GAR 96]), especially in Mathematics. For this reason, educational games create a mental disposition that makes the student concentrate without getting involved with the world around them, making learning constant for a certain period of time.

In the application of the considered games, Figure 16 reveals the students' taste about the educational games. The game Math in the Jungle showed 50% (fifty percent) satisfaction by the students, while in the game Tangram 21% (twenty one percent) of the students liked the involvement generated by the manipulation of geometric shapes. In TuxMath and 29% (twenty nine percent) are satisfied with the game.

---

5 Maturity, According to **Piaget** (1987), the origin of cognitive development is from the inside to the outside, occurring according to the **maturity of** the person.

6 Intelligence, intelligence is not one, but consists of a set of relatively independent abilities. Psychologist Howard Gardner developed the Theory of multiple intelligences by dividing intelligence into seven different components: logical-mathematical, linguistic, spatial, musical, kinematic, intra-personal and inter-personal.

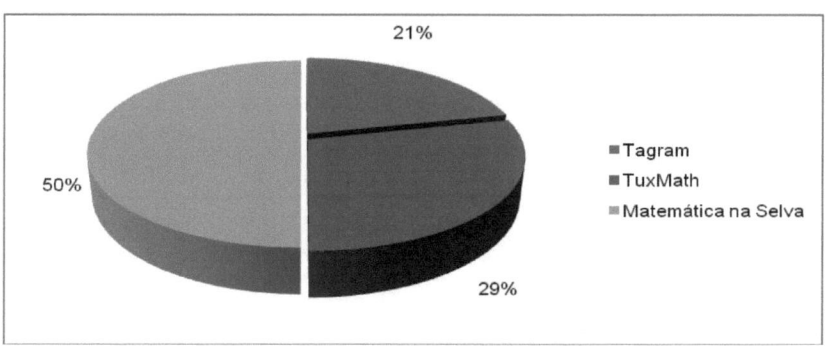

Figure 16: A taste for educational play.

The graph presented in Figure 17 illustrates that what most caught the students' attention in the Tangram game were the runaways (central point of the game). The game does not present questions or accounts so did not get percentage in these areas. In the survey, 10% (ten percent) of the students were very curious about the sound the game made when forming the figures; 16% (sixteen percent) agreed that the colours caught their attention; for 33% (thirty-three percent) the attention was focused on the scenery that dazzled them when they noticed the geometric shapes; finally, 41% (forty-one percent) appreciated the figures that should be formed. In the game it was observed that perception, concentration and attention stimulated the visual by absorbing the shapes and contours of the geometric figure format.

Figure 17 reveals the events that drew more attention presented in the graph of the game Tangram as colours, scenery, figures, questions and sound. This shows that the perception and fundamental to be able to increase the concentration, the motivation of students before the situations proposed by what is showing the game. This conveys that the teacher observes his goal is really being achieved by the students are demonstrating when running the games.

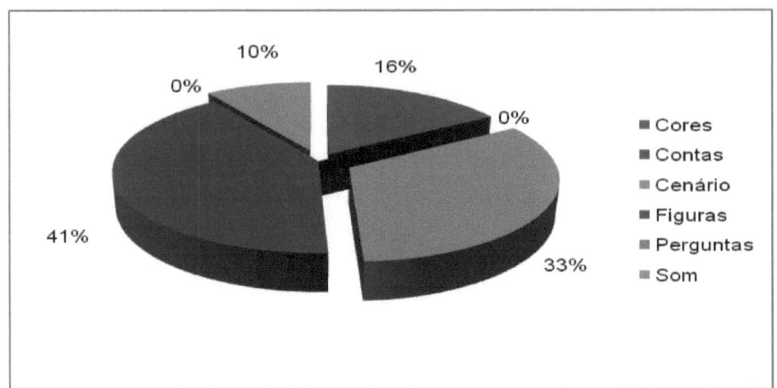

Figure 17: The events that caught the most attention in the Tangram game.

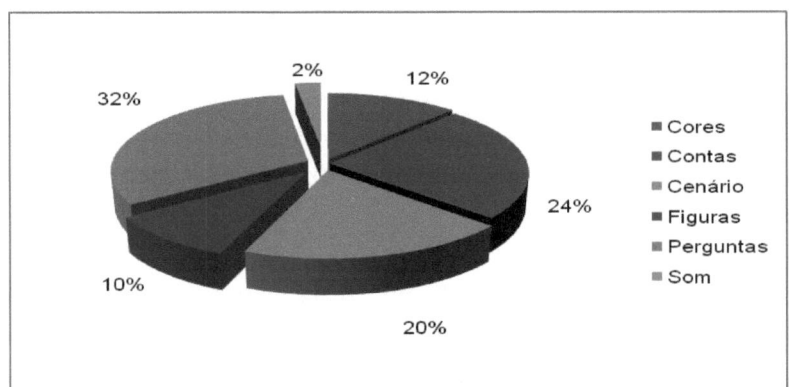

Figure 18: The events that caught the most attention in the TuxMath game.

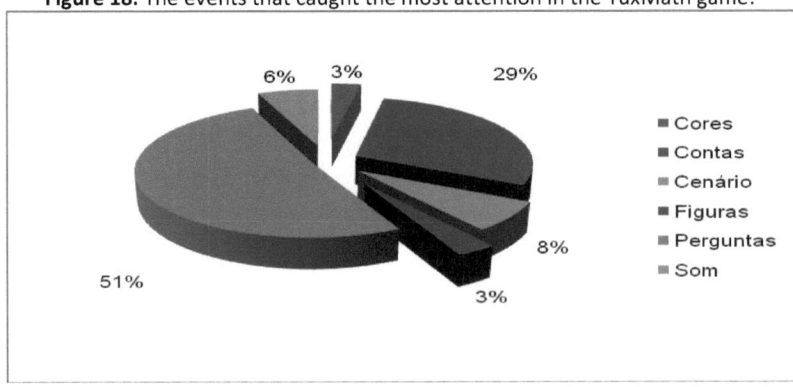

Figure 19: The events that most caught your attention in the Maths in the Jungle game.

48

Figure 18 shows the status of events that caught the students' attention with regards to the game. The graph indicates the percentage of each point that was revealed above in the TuxMath game 32% (thirty-two percent) of respondents what caught their attention most was the way the questions were designed, 24% (twenty-four percent) the maths, 20% (twenty percent) the scenario was very attractive, 12% (twelve percent) the colours presented in the game, 10% (ten percent) was the pictures and 2% noticed that the sound held their attention to the games.

The graph in figure 19 shows what happened when the students started to manipulate the Math in the Jungle game what called out were the questions with a percentage of 51% (fifty one percent), 29% (twenty nine percent) the maths, 8% (eight percent) the scenario, 3% (three percent) the colours, 3% (three percent) the figures and 6% (six percent) the sound that when played emitted soft sound that greatly contributed to drawing the attention of the students to what it was showing in what was really the operations.

In the figure 20 presents the difficulties that occurred in the game Tangram when manipulating the game directly on the computer by the students that 58% (fifty eight percent) answered the survey that had difficulty in running the game and that 42% (forty two percent) found no difficulty when they start show the geometric form presented by the educational game.

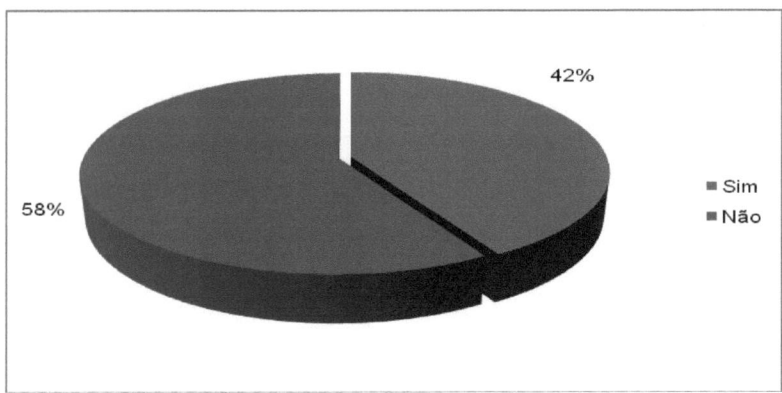

Figure 20: Difficulties in the Tangram game.

The difficulties presented by students in playing the TuxMath game is revealed in Figure 21. By the percentage expressed, 25% (twenty percent) of the respondents agreed that the educational game has its operations as a hindering factor; 75% (seventy-five percent) see no obstacles when answering the mathematical accounts and the speed that it is presented.

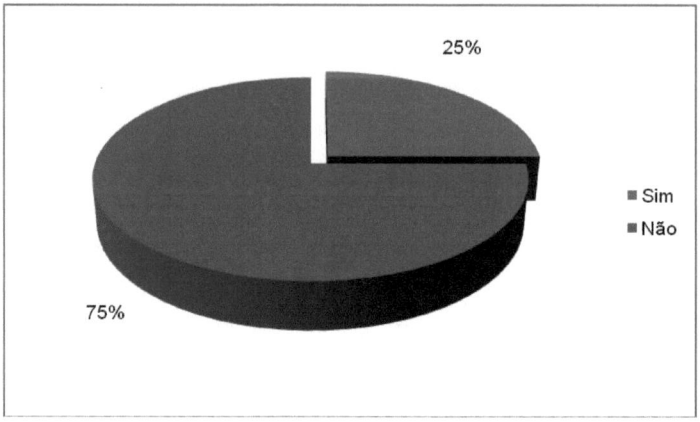

25%

75%

■ Sim
■ Não

Figure 21: Difficulties in the TuxMath game.

Figure 22 shows the graph relating to the difficulties encountered with the game Mathematics in the Jungle. In the results it can be seen that 57% (fifty-seven percent) had a lot of difficulty in relation to what the game Mathematics in the Jungle, because it works with a more in-depth Mathematics, such as exponentiation[7]. However, 43% (forty-three percent) excelled when faced with operations.

---

7 Exponentiation or potentiation is a unary operation used in arithmetic to indicate the multiplication of a given base by itself as many times as the exponent indicates, and is the opposite mathematical operation to radiciation.

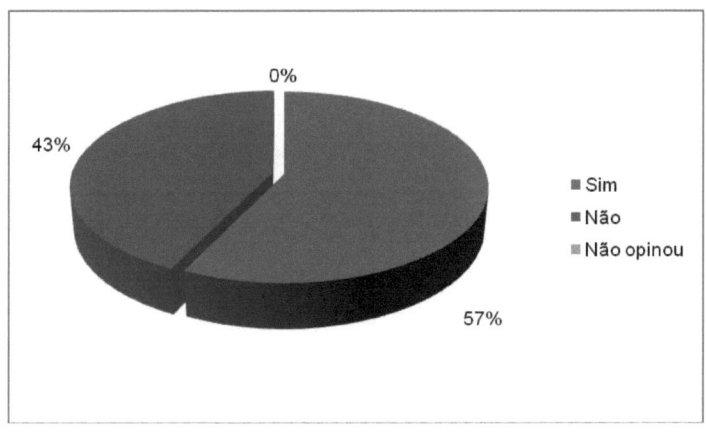

Figure 22: Difficulties in the Maths in the Jungle game.

Figure 23 shows the data about the challenges addressed in the Tangram game. Unfortunately 55% (fifty-five percent) of the respondents answered the poll saying that they had an obstacle in assembling the geometric figures. This is probably due to the fact that the students did not enjoy the game. Of the remaining respondents, 18% (eighteen percent) did not understand the execution of the game felt challenged and 27% (twenty seven percent) agreed that in the game I did not have challenging.

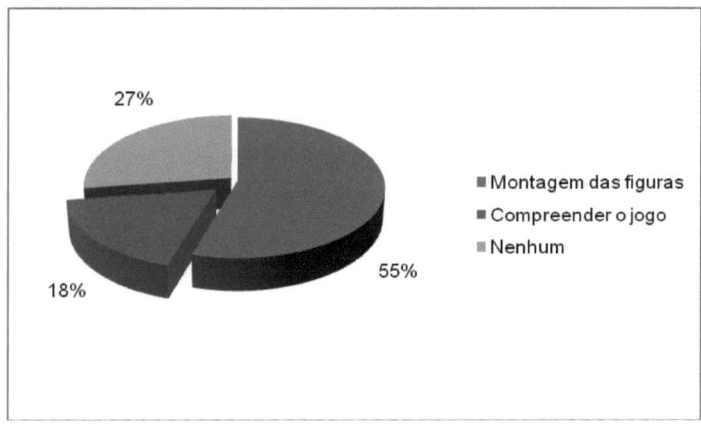

Figure 23: You felt challenged by the Tangram game.

The challenges found in the TuxMath game aim to identify the learner's level of knowledge of mathematical operations, which can measure skills, concentration and motivation. Figure 24 shows that 43% of the respondents had difficulty with the speed with which the game was played, 41% found the game challenging when faced with mathematical expressions of fundamental operations, 8% of the pupils found it difficult to play the game as a whole, and 8% did not find the game challenging at all.

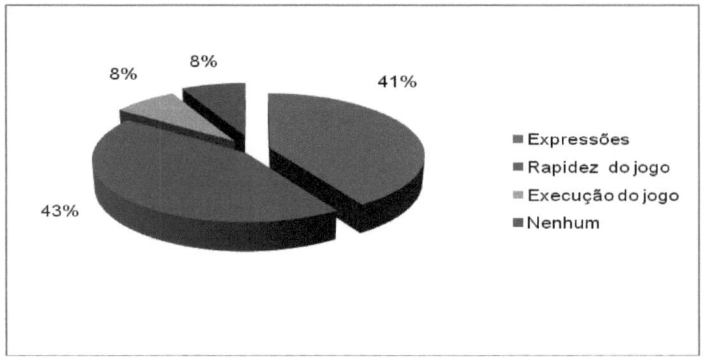

Figure 24: You felt challenged by the TuxMath game.

Figure 25 deals with the challenges found in the Math in the Jungle game. Of the respondents, 50% (fifty percent) did not rate the game as challenging. However, this shows that the students are learning what is being presented in the classroom. Thirty-eight percent (38%) said they had a lot of difficulty in playing the game and eight percent (8%) did not respond to the survey. The difficulty is due to the fact that students do not have practice with expressions or because they really do not know the subject.

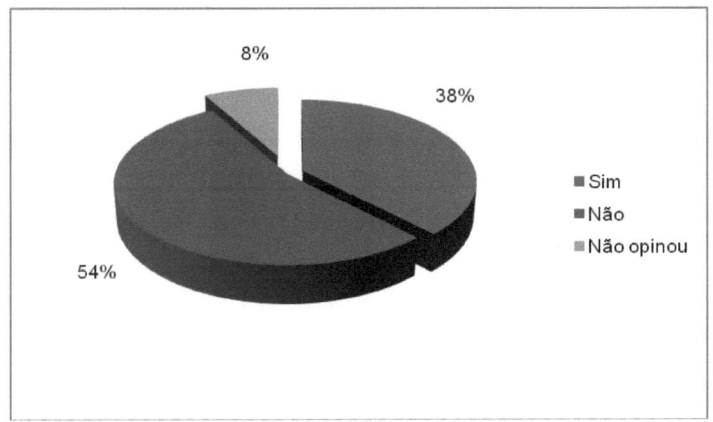

Figure 25: Did you feel challenged by the Maths in the Jungle game.

Regarding the grades from zero to ten (0 to 10), the students evaluated the educational games according to what was presented and it was found that 51% (fifty one percent) colours gave the gradeten, 48% (forty eight percent) scenario gave the grade ten, 1% (one percent) hints gave the grade ten and for exercises gave grades not expressive for research the grades had a balance between zero to nine in all points presented in the game revealed in Figure 26.

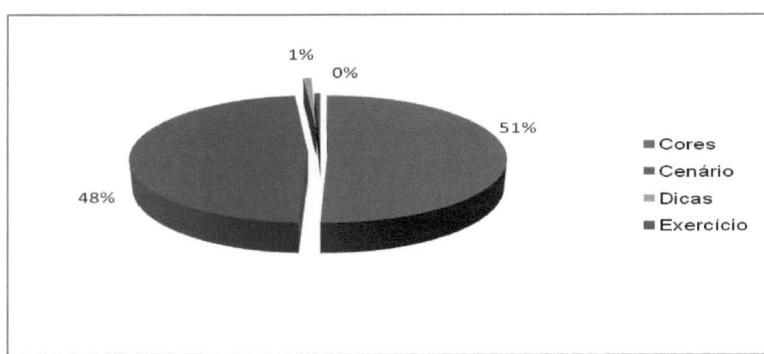

Figure 26: Score of the three games.

The Figures ensureir present the percentage of what the students liked most addressed in the games.

53

Figures 27, 28 and 29 show the features that most attracted the students to the Tangram game, i.e. colours, landscapes and hints respectively. The graphs reveal the importance of colours in the Tangram game, where 83% (eighty-three percent) responded that their attention was drawn to the colours, while only 17% (seventeen percent) saw no importance of colours for learning the operations.

Regarding the landscapes, Figure 27 reveals that 50% (fifty percent) of the interviewed students were not attracted by the environment presented in the game, while 50% (fifty percent) positively agreed that they liked the game with its way of transmitting the mathematics content. As Tangram is a game that requires a lot of geometric notion, 83% agreed that the hints in the game are important, with only 17% not needing hints.

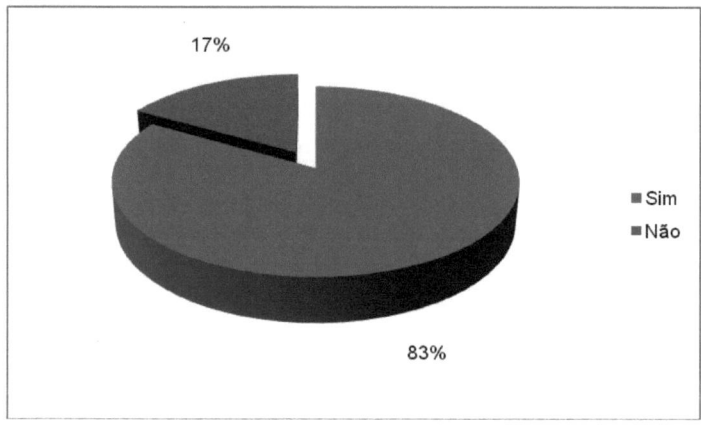

Figure 27: The taste for colours used in the Tangram game.

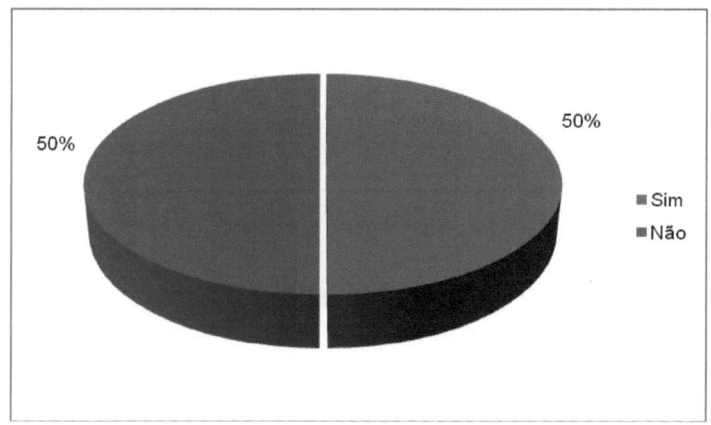

Figure 28: A taste for landscapes in the Tangram game.

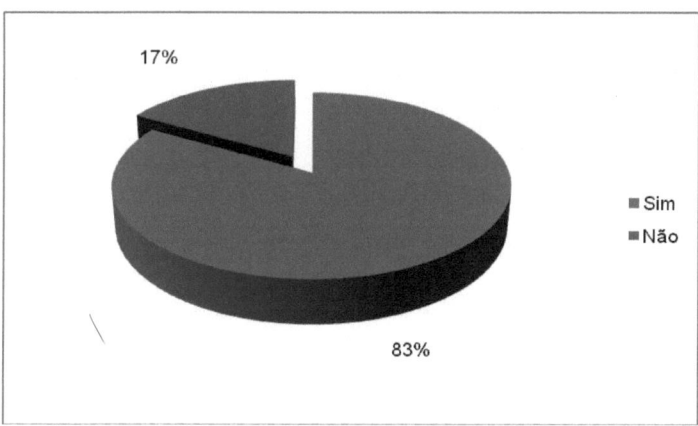

Figure 29: The taste for "hints" in the Tangram game.

In the TuxMath game it was observed that 100% of the students saw the environment as positive. Regarding the tips Figure 30 shows that 75% liked the tips and 15% did not care for them.

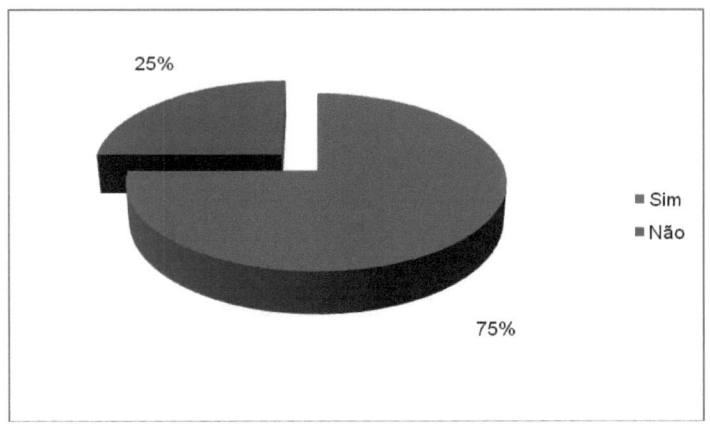

25%

■ Sim
■ Não

75%

Figure 30: A taste for "hints" in the TuxMath game.

Figure 31 reveals the students' liking for the TuxMath game in terms of percentage 31% (thirty one percent) of the respondents find the colours attractive, 28% (twenty eight percent) liked the exercises presented by the game, 26% (twenty six percent) the scenario and 15% (fifteen percent) the tips were fundamental to overcome the obstacles presented in the educational game. The concentration for the success of the approach that the game presents is to draw attention to the steps that the game shows when handled by the player.

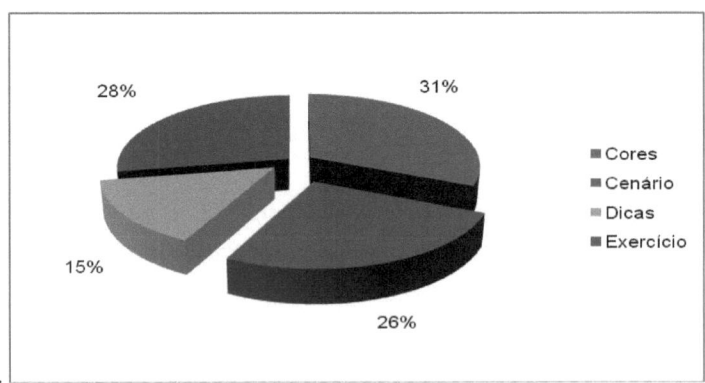

28%   31%

■ Cores
■ Cenário
■ Dicas
■ Exercício

15%

26%

Figure 31: What you liked about the TuxMath game.

In relation to the Maths in the Jungle game, the graph in Figure 32 indicates that there was a good acceptance of the exercises presented by the game, that is, 93% (ninety-three percent) liked the way the exercises were worked. Only 7% (seven percent) were not productive with the exercises presented.

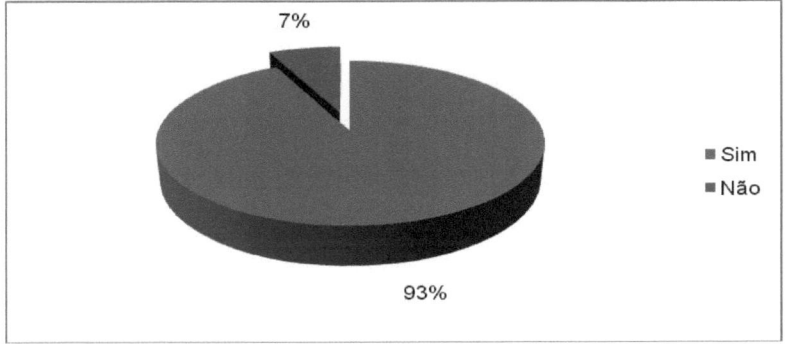

Figure 32: The enjoyment of the "exercises" in the Maths in the Jungle game.

After getting to know the games the interviewees were asked what they would change about the games used. Figure 33 shows the results for the game Tangram. A percentage of 17% (seventeen percent) would not change the profile of Tangram, 16% (sixteen percent) would change the game due to complexity, 17% (seventeen percent) of respondents would change the way it is prepared the calculation questions presented in the game itself, 17% (seventeen percent) of students, in this process, would choose another game to perform the activities and 33% (thirty-three percent) of respondents had no opinion.

What makes the game exciting in the teaching-learning process is to solve the exposed problems so that the player can change phase.

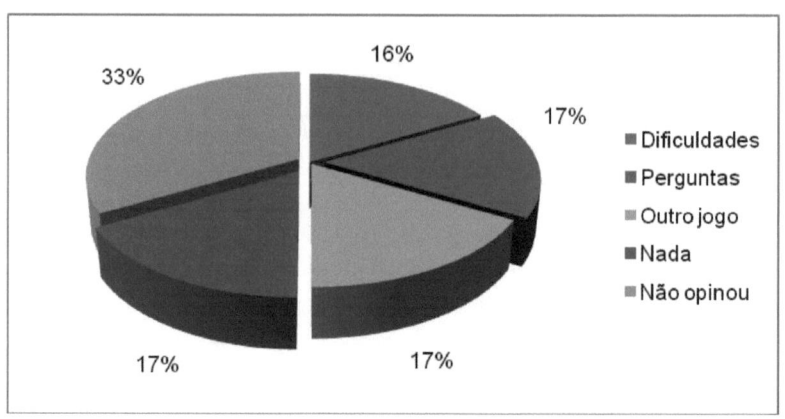

Figure 33: Change would occur in the Tangram game.

Figure 34 shows the changes that students would make to the TuxMath game. 50% (fifty percent) of the students interviewed agree with the way the game was presented and that no changes are needed to understand its dynamics, but 12% (twelve percent) observe that the maths needs to be improved, 25% (twenty-five percent) the questions addressed and 13% (thirteen percent) reported that there was insufficient time to manipulate the game.

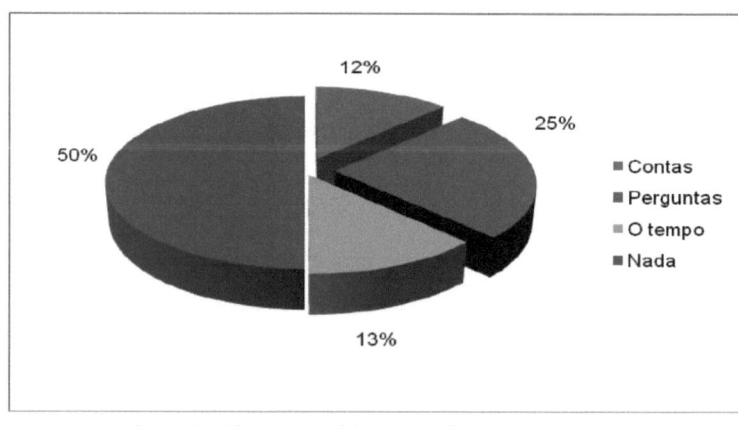

Figure 34: Change would occur in the game TuxMath.

Finally, the graph shown in Figure 35 translates what the students answered about what would change in the game Math in the Jungle. The percentage presented is 50% (fifty percent) for students who agreed that the way the game is is ideal for good learning, 15% (fifteen percent) think that changes should be made to the figures in the scenario, 14% (fourteen percent) determined that the questions could be reformulated, 7% (seven percent) would like the expressions to be made easier and 14% (fourteen percent) did not answer the poll presented in the questionnaire.

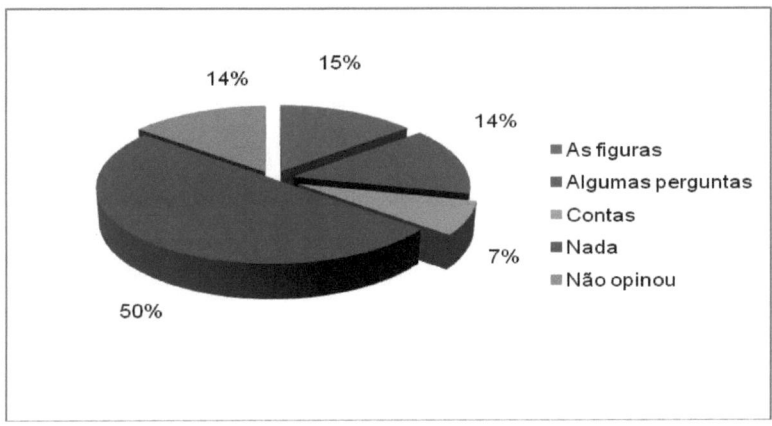

Figure 35: Change would occur in the Math in the Jungle game.

The graphs reveal what really learning takes place in the educational field in the lives of students in the use of the computer as a tool in the teaching learning process to link to another subject facilitating complexity as in the case of Mathematics.

And the graphs presented portray the reality experienced in the computer lab using the operating system Educational Linux.

Figure 36: Students in the lab   **Figure 37:** Students at work

Figures 36 and 37 show the laboratory with the students carrying out the research regarding the questionnaire revealed by the percentage data presented by the graphs.

7 FINAL CONSIDERATIONS

The contribution about the usefulness of educational computer games in the teaching-learning process is wide and of great importance for the improvement of mathematics teaching, either in the school "Aluísio Azevedo" Teaching Centre or in other institutions.

With the changes in the pedagogical paradigm and the emergence of new technologies, such as the computer and the Internet, teachers opened the doors to the use of resources that go beyond the traditional vision and the merely discursive methods in the teaching-learning process. Thus, with the growth of Educational Technology, the educational games were configured as a complementary tool in the construction and fixation of concepts developed in the classroom, as well as a motivating resource for both the teacher and the student.

The implementation of easy-to-use software, such as Math in the Jungle, Tangram and TuxMath, makes teachers interested in the applicability of educational games directly in the classroom. Thus, it is believed that, little by little, this type of educational software, available in the market, will have its quality increased with respect to its pedagogical character, resulting in an increase in the productivity of students facing the subject that they are studying.

Both the students and the teachers showed interest in the games presented, and the important factor in this work was the encouragement of the female audience with computer games. Another important fact detected is that colours, landscapes and hints can draw attention to the games being a motivating factor.

Efforts are being made to offer new options for animations and colours in games.

One problem detected is that students at the school in question do not have technology in their homes, and have partial (or no) access to computers.

In addition, computer labs are not targets for this type of educational activity, or else the school works with restricted financial resources.

Although these problems have been detected, it could be observed that computer games for education develop a motivating, attractive and captivating environment in which students feel stimulated by obstacles and consequently acquire knowledge through playful activities.

8 REFERENCES

ANTUNES, Celso. **A avaliação da aprendizagem escolar**. 3rd ed. Petrópolis: Artmed, 2003.

AUSUBEL, D. P. 1968. **Educational psychology : a cognitive view.** New York: Holt, Rinehart and Winston.

BARBOSA, Laura Monte Serrat. **Projeto de trabalho: uma forma de atuação psicopedagógica**. 2.ed. Curitiba: L. M. S, 1998.

BATTAIOLA, A.L. **Jogos por computador - histórico, relevância tecnológica e mercadológica, tendências e técnicas** de **implementação**, In: XIX JORNADA DE ATUALIZAÇÃO EM INFORMÁTICA. Anaisdo XIX Congresso Nacional da SBC. Curitiba: PUCPR, 2000.

CARVALHO, Raimundo da Ressurreição Chagas. **Atualização para Windows XP**. Caxias-Ma: Proinf, 2005.

DAVIDOFF, L.L. **Introdução à Psicologia**. 3a. ed. São Paulo: Makron Books, 2001.

DEMO, P. **Avaliação Qualitativa**. Cortez Editora e Editora Autores Associados, 1941.

FAGUNDES, L.; Sato, L.S.; Maçada, D.L. **Aprendizes do Futuro: as inovações começaram**. MEC, Porto Alegre, 1998.

FARIA, Anália Rodrigues de. **O desenvolvimento da criança e do adolescente segundo Piaget**. Ed. Ática, 3rd edition, 1995.

GARDNER, Howard. **Structures of the Mind - The theory of Multiple Intelligences**. Ed. Artes Médicas, 1996.

GONÇALVES, Hortência de Abreu. **Manual de projetos de pesquisa científica**. São Paulo: Avercamp, 2003.

LEIF, J. and Brunelle, L. **O jogo pelo jogo**. Rio de Janeiro, Zahar, 1978.

LIMA, M.F.W.P, ; TAROUCO, L.M.R. **Análise da Conduta de Professores e Alunos em Enientes Digitais Virtuais.** In: XIV SIMPÓSIO BRASILEIRO DE INFORMÁTICA NA EDUCAÇÃO. Annals of the XIV Brazilian Symposium of Computer Science in Education. Rio de Janeiro: NCE/RJ, 2003.

MARTINS, J. G.; MOCO, S. S.; MARTINS, A. R.; BARCIA, R. M. **Virtual Reality through Games in Education.** Universidade Federal de Santa Catarina. Graduate Program in Production Engineering. 2001.

PASSERINO, L.M. **Avaliação de jogos educativos computadorizados.** Taller Internacional de Software Educacional 1988. Santiago (Chile).

School learning and the construction of knowledge. 2nd ed. Porto Alegre: Artes Médicas, 1994.

SILVEIRA, R. S; BARONE, D. A. C. **Educational computer games using the genetic algorithms approach.** Federal University of Rio Grande do Sul. Instituto de Informática. Graduate Course in Computer Science. 1998.

RAUEN, Fábio José. **Elemento de iniciação à pesquisa.** São Luís, MA: UEMA and NEAD, 2006.

RIZZZI, Leonor and Haydt, Regina Célia. **Atividades lúdicas na educação da criança.** Ed. Ática, 6th edition, Série Educação. 1997.

ZABALA, Antoni. **A prática educativa: Como ensinar.** Porto Alegre: ArtMed, 1998.

Educational Games applied to e-Learning: changing the way students are assessed. Available at http://www.abed.org.br/seminario2003/texto21.htm. Accessed from the Teleduc Support Material on 13/12/2008.

Tangram Educational Game. Available at http://pt.wikipedia.org/wiki/Tangram. Accessed on 03/10/2008.

TuxMath Educational Game. Available at http://superdownloads.uol.com.br/download/139/tuxmath-linux/. Accessed on 03/12/2008.

Mathematics in the Jungle Educational Game. Available at www.universitariojundiai.g12.br . **Accessed on 03/10/2008.**

Educational Games. Available at http://www.ueb-df.org.br/artigo.asp?art=36. Accessed on 13/10/2008.

PASSERINO, L.M. **Avaliação de jogos educativos computadorizados.** Taller Internacional de Software Educativo 1998. Santiago (Chile). Retrieved from: http://www.c5.cl/tise98/html/trabajos/jogosed/ on 13 February 2009.

Piaget and genetic epistemology. Available at http://teleduc.cinted.ufrgs.br/~teleduc/cursos/aplic/index.php?cod_curso=890_3/ /piaget..... Accessed from the Teleduc support material on 03/10/2008.

Rieder, Rafael, **Observation and Analysis of the Application of Two Dimensional Educational Games in an Open Environment.** Available at http://teleduc.cinted.ufrgs.br/~teleduc/cursos/aplic/index.php?cod_course=890... . Accessed from the Teleduc support material on 03/10/2008.

TAROUCO, Liane, **Games, computer and Internet in education.** Available at http://penta3.ufrgs.br/animacoes/JogosEducacionais. Accessed from the Teleduc Support Material on 13/02/2009.

TAROUCO, L. **Jogos Educacionais. Journal New Technologies in Education.** V.2 N.1, March, 2004. CINTED/UFRGS. Porto Alegre-RS. Available at: http://www.cinted.ufrgs.br/renote/. Accessed on February 2009

VYGOSTKY, L. S. **A formação social da mente.** São Paulo: Martins Fontes, 1988.

APPENDICES

FEDERAL UNIVERSITY OF RIO GRANDE DO SUL

INTERDISCIPLINARY CENTRE FOR NEW TECHNOLOGIES IN EDUCATION

INFORMATION TECHNOLOGIES FOR EDUCATORS

RESEARCH: EDUCATIONAL GAMES: A Learning Approach to Mathematics Teaching
TARGET AUDIENCE: TEACHERS.

01. Vocational training:

(   ) University Course. What _____Institution:
_____

(   ) Post-Graduation. Which
_____

(   ) Finished   ( ) Studying

02. How many years have you been a professional in the field?

(   ) 0 year to 1 year
(   ) between 1 and 5 years
(   ) between 6 and 9 years old
(   ) more than 10 years

03. How is your knowledge of computers?
( )   excellent   (   ) regular   (   ) little   (   ) no knowledge

04. Do you have knowledge about computer games?
(   ) no   (   ) yes   (   ) regular

05. In your opinion, the application of educational games in a discipline:

(   ) is fundamental to increase the concentration and learning power of the student

(   ) increases the student's difficulties in learning a certain

subject

(   ) cannot be used in the classroom by the teacher

(   ) leaves the student alienated.

06. Do you consider the educational games important in the teaching-learning process?

(   ) yes   (   ) no

07. How do you rate the qualifications of the computer science teacher?

(   ) Important for the teaching-learning process

(   ) no importance

(   ) there is no restriction anyone can work

08. Do you have any knowledge about any educational games aimed at education?

(   ) yes   (   ) no

09. What do you consider important for the appropriate use of games in the computer lab with secondary school students?

(   ) knowledge of basic computing

(   ) knowledge about the games presented in Educational Linux

( ) knowledge about internet, software

10. How would you qualify the work developed at school regarding the use of educational games?

( )   good   (   ) very good   (   ) excellent   ( ) no knowledge

11. What do you think about the use of the computer in learning with educational games that aim to motivate, increase the power of concentration, thus favouring the resolution of activities?

( )   good   (   ) very good   (   ) excellent   (   ) bad

12. Have you ever applied an educational game in your class?

(   ) yes   (   ) no

13. Have you ever used a computer game outside the classroom?

( ) yes   ( ) no   If yes, what is the game? _____

FEDERAL UNIVERSITY OF RIO GRANDE DO SUL

INTERDISCIPLINARY CENTRE FOR NEW TECHNOLOGIES IN EDUCATION

INFORMATION TECHNOLOGIES FOR EDUCATORS

RESEARCH: EDUCATIONAL GAMES: A Learning Approach to Mathematics Teaching
TARGET AUDIENCE: STUDENTS

1. Name of the game:

_____

_____

2. Series:

_____

3. The name of the School:

( ) Municipal   ( ) Federal   ( ) State   ( ) Private

4. Sex:

(   ) M   (   ) F

5. Date of birth:

6. Did you enjoy the game? Why did you like it?

_____

_____

_____

7. What were the events that most caught your attention in the game?

_____

_____

_____

8. How long did it take you to run the game?

_____
_____
_____
_____

9. Did you experience any difficulties when playing the game?

_____
_____
_____
_____

10. What challenge did you face when running the game?

_____
_____
_____

11. Give a score from zero to ten (0 to 10) for each item below:

    (   ) Colors   (   ) Scenery   (   ) Exercise   ( ) Tips

12. Which of the items below did you like?

    (   ) Colors   (   ) Scenery   (   ) Exercise   ( ) Tips

13. What would you change about the game?

_____
_____
_____

14. Did you like the colours?

    (   ) yes   (   ) no

15. Did you like the landscapes (atmosphere of the game)?

( ) yes   (   ) no

16. Did you like the tips, and reminders that appeared in the game?

    (   ) yes   (   ) no

17. Did you like the exercises presented by the game?

    (   ) yes   (   ) no

SCHOOL: "Aluísio Azevedo" Teaching Centre   LOCALITY: Av. Francisco Castro, S/N, Ponte
DISCIPLINE: Computing   DURATION OF CLASS: 50 min.
GRADE: 1st Grade
TEACHER:

LESSON PLAN

OBJECTIVES	CONTENTS	PROCEDURES	TEACHING RESOURCES	EVALUATION

Bibliography: